Investigate Science

Air Is Everywhere

by Melissa Stewart

Content Adviser: Jan Jenner, Ph.D.

Science Adviser: Terrence E. Young Jr., M.Ed., M.L.S., Jefferson Parish (La.) Public Schools

Reading Adviser: Rosemary G. Palmer, Ph.D., Department of Literacy, College of Education, Boise State University

COMPASS POINT BOOKS ✦ MINNEAPOLIS, MINNESOTA

Compass Point Books
3109 West 50th St., #115
Minneapolis, MN 55410

Visit Compass Point Books on the Internet at *www.compasspointbooks.com* or e-mail your request to *custserv@compasspointbooks.com*

Creative Director: Terri Foley
Managing Editor: Catherine Neitge
Editors: Nadia Higgins, Christianne C. Jones
Photo Researcher: Svetlana Zhurkina
Designer: The Design Lab
Illustrator: Jeffrey Scherer
Educational Consultant: Diane Smolinski

Library of Congress Cataloging-in-Publication Data
Stewart, Melissa.
Air is everywhere / by Melissa Stewart.
   p. cm. — (Investigate science)
Summary: Introduces the characteristics and importance of air through text, illustrations, and activities.
Includes bibliographical references and index.
ISBN 0-7565-0638-7 (hardcover)
1. Air—Juvenile literature. [1. Air.] I. Title. II. Series.
QC161.2.S73 2004
533'.6—dc22   2003022715

Note to Readers: To learn about the air, scientists do experiments. They write about everything they observe. They make charts and drawings.

This book will help you study air the way a scientist does. To get started, you will need a notebook and a pencil.

In the Doing More section in the back of the book, you will find step-by-step instructions for some more fun science experiments and activities.

In this book, words that are defined in the glossary are in **bold** the first time they appear in the text.

Table of Contents

Where Is Air?   4

Floating on Air   13

The Power of Air   14

We Need Air   21

Doing More   26

Explanations to Questions   30

Glossary   31

To Find Out More   31

Index   32

As you read this book, be on the lookout for these special symbols:

 Ask an adult for help.

Turn to the back of the book for another activity.

Go to page 30 for an explanation to a question.

Where Is Air?

Air blows at the playground and everywhere else you go.

Wherever you go, **air** is all around you. Air fills your home. It seeps inside the tiniest cracks. Air blows at the park. It flows through the sky. You can't see air, but you can feel it.

Hold your hand in front of your mouth and blow out. What does air feel like as it leaves your body?

Now go to a large open area and run as fast as you can. Can you feel air pressing against your skin? Place a piece of paper against your stomach and run some more. The paper stays flat against you. It doesn't fall because air holds it in place.

Let's do some experiments and see what else we can find out about the air around us.

When you run, you can feel air moving against your skin.

Air inside a basketball makes it bounce.

6

You Can Tell There's Air Inside a Bag

Even when you can't feel air, there are ways to tell it's there. Tear up a sheet of paper into many pieces, and drop the pieces into a clear, plastic bag. Gather up the bag's opening in one hand. Then slip a straw into the opening and blow. Hold your hand tight around the straw and bag. What happens? How do you know there's air in the bag?

?
See Explanation

See page 30 for an answer.

There's also air inside a bicycle's tires and a basketball. Without air, you couldn't ride to the playground for a game of hoops! Draw pictures of three other things that need to be filled with air.

What you need:
• a sheet of paper
• a clear, plastic bag
• a drinking straw

Air pumps up a bike's tires.

7

What you need:
- a sink
- a glass
- a napkin

Air takes up space that isn't filled by other things. It's inside an oven, a waste basket, and even an empty glass.

To see the air inside an empty drinking glass, fill up your kitchen sink with water. Get a glass that is shorter than the sink and that you can see through. Then stuff a napkin into the glass. Turn the glass upside down, and carefully lower it straight into the sink. Lower the glass all the way so that the water covers it.

Do you think the napkin will get wet? Keeping the glass upside-down, lift it out of the water and see. The glass is full of air, so water can't get inside. Air keeps the napkin dry!

Stuff the napkin into the bottom of a clear glass.

Keep the glass straight as you lower it into the sink.

Water covered the glass, but the napkin stayed dry!

9

Think of all the places you see bubbles in water.

Make Bubbles Rise in Water

You can catch a glimpse of air in motion.
Take the napkin out of the glass. Carefully
lower the glass into the water
again. Then slowly tip the glass
onto its side.

Draw a picture of what
you see. The **bubbles** escaping
from the glass are full of air.

Can you guess why
air bubbles rise in water?
See page 30 for the answer.

See Explanation

See page 30 for the answer.

What you need:
• a sink
• a glass

When you tip the
glass to the
side, air bubbles
come out.

11

Balloons filled
with helium gas
soar into the sky.

Floating on Air

What Makes a Balloon Float or Sink?

Have you ever seen birthday balloons rise up to the ceiling? Those balloons were filled with helium **gas.** Helium weighs less than air, which is a mixture of other gases. So helium-filled balloons **float.** What about a balloon that you blow up yourself?

Ask an Adult

Blow up a balloon, and ask an adult to help you tie it. Now let the balloon go, and observe what happens. Does it float?

Unlike helium, the air you blew into the balloon weighs the same as the air all around it. However, the rubber balloon itself is heavier than air. The balloon sinks to the floor.

What you need:
• a balloon to blow up

Why will this balloon sink to the ground?

The Power of Air

Observe Wind's Power

Did you know that **wind** is just gusts of air moving up and down? When air warms up, it spreads out and gets thinner and lighter than cool air. When the sun heats up the air near the ground, that warm air rises in the sky. Cooler air moves down to take its place. As warm air moves up and cold air moves down, wind blows.

Wind makes trees sway and flags flap. What else can wind do? Stand outside on a windy day. Notice all the things wind can move. Look far away and close by. Look up and down. Make a list of everything you observe. For more activities about wind, see pages 26 and 28.

You can see wind's power all around you.

14

Did You Know?

Wind farms are fields with rows and rows of windmills. The windmills help turn the power of wind into electricity.

Spoon the runny paint on a sheet of paper.

Use a Drinking Straw to Paint

Air can do other amazing things besides create wind. When you blow air through a drinking straw, you can make some really great art.

Ask an Adult

Ask an adult to help you add extra water to your favorite paint. Place two spoonfuls of watery paint on a white sheet of paper. Then use a straw to create some fun designs. What happens to the paint when you blow gently? When you blow hard?

You can paint using only a straw and your breath.

17

What you need:
- a balloon
- a bicycle pump
- a rubber band
- a heavy book
- a ruler

Would you believe that air has the power to lift a book? To see what air can do, stretch the opening of a balloon around the hose of a bicycle pump. Wrap a rubber band around the neck of the balloon so the hose can't slip out. Put a heavy book, such as a dictionary, on top of the balloon.

Start pumping air into the balloon. How high can you lift the book? Use a ruler to measure how far the book lifts off the floor. Try the experiment two more times, and keep track of your measurements in your notebook. Do you get the same results each time?

Stretch the balloon to make a tight seal around the hose of the bicycle pump.

As the balloon
fills up, the
book rises.

Your breath keeps you alive, and it lets you do some fun things, too.

We Need Air

How Long Can You Hold Your Breath?

Think of all the things you need to keep your body healthy. You need food, water, and a place to live. You also need air. Every time you breathe in, fresh air enters your body. When you breathe out, used air leaves your body.

You can live a month without food and more than a week without water, but you can survive only a few minutes without air. Use a stopwatch or a clock to find out how long you can hold your breath. Now test a friend, and compare your results. Do the experiment two more times, and write your results in your notebook.

For another experiment on breathing, see page 29.

What you need:
• a stopwatch or clock with a second hand

You can hold your breath for only a minute or two.

21

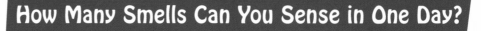

How Many Smells Can You Sense in One Day?

Go outside and take a deep breath. Can you tell if someone has just mowed the lawn? Are your neighbors having a barbecue? When you breathe, your nose does more than take in air. It also smells.

Air is important because it helps you smell. Tiny specks of food, perfume, and smoke can float in the air. Air carries those specks to your nose.

How many different smells do you think your nose picks up in a day? Five, 10, 100? Tomorrow, keep a list of everything you smell. How many different smells are carried in the air around you?

Close your eyes and concentrate on all the smells in the air.

Your nose senses tiny bits of food in the air.

Air carries invisible sound waves that ripple away from a drum.

Experiment with Your Hearing

Air also lets you hear things. When someone beats a drum, waves of sound ripple away from the drum. Air gives those sound waves something to ripple *through*. Air carries sound waves to your ears, and you hear the drumbeat.

Your ears catch sound waves and send them inside your head. Predict what would happen if you had larger ears. To find out, cup your hands behind your ears and listen carefully. Now listen without your hands. Do your hands make things sound different? Why? See page 30 for an answer.

Now that you've examined air, you know that it can do many things. Look, feel, smell, listen. Take a deep breath. You can sense air's power all around you.

People sometimes cup their ears to hear better.

Big ears give a bat-eared fox excellent hearing.

25

Make a Kite

On page 14, you learned that wind is moving air. You made a list of all the things wind can move. Was flying kites on your list? Here's a way to make your own kite:

1. Find a sheet of regular typing paper or construction paper. Fold it in half as shown in illustration 1.

2. Then fold it diagonally as shown in illustration 2.

3. You now have one triangle folded over another. Unfold the bottom triangle. You now have a diamond shape over a triangle shape (the same triangle that used to be on top). A fold runs the long way through the middle of the diamond. Tape this fold to the paper beneath it, as shown in illustration 3.

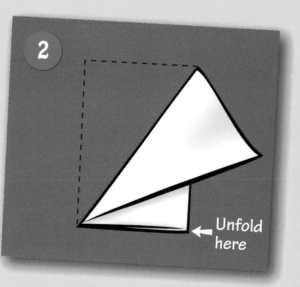

Unfold here

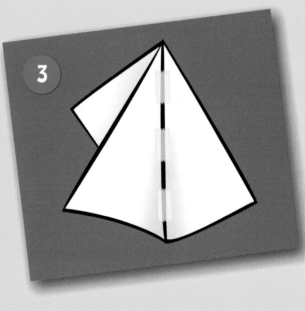

4. Tape a plastic drinking straw across the paper as shown in illustration 4. Secure the straw at both ends.

5. Pick up the kite and turn it sideways. Ask an adult to help you punch a hole toward the front of the kite's bottom flap (underneath the straw). Get a piece of string at least 3 feet (90 centimeters) long. Tie one end of the string around the hole. Now tape strips of newspaper to the back end of the flap to make a tail. Your kite should look like illustration 5.

6. Now take your kite outside. Hold the string in one hand and lift the kite high above your head with the other hand. When the kite catches a breeze, let go and tug on the string. Does your kite fly? Try flying your kite in different places around your neighborhood. Where does your kite fly best?

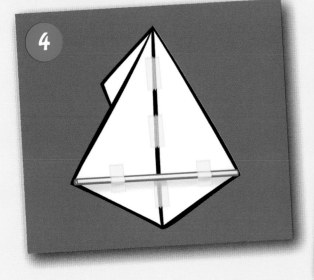

Make a Miniature Sailboat

On pages 14 and 15, you learned that wind can be powerful. Wind turns windmills that make electricity. Powerful wind also pushes sailboats across lakes. You can make a miniature sailboat that you power with your breath.

Ask an Adult

1. Ask an adult to help you punch a hole in each end of an index card. The index card will be the sail of your boat. Now slip a plastic drinking straw through the two holes. The straw is your boat's mast.

2. Tape one end of the straw to the inside of the lid from a peanut butter or mayonnaise jar. The lid is the hull, or main body, of your boat. Your boat should look like the one in the illustration.

3. The next time you take a bath, test out your sailboat. Blow on the index card. What happens? You may need to add a little weight, such as a penny, to help balance your boat. Try blowing from different angles. Which angle makes the boat move fastest? Now blow on the index card through another plastic straw. Does the boat move faster or slower?

What Affects People's and Animals' Breathing?

On page 21, you learned just how important air is for keeping us alive. To learn more about breathing, try these experiments.

1. Use a clock or a stopwatch to find out how many breaths you take each minute. Then run for five minutes, and try again. Do you get a different answer?

2. Repeat this experiment on three other people. Try to test some older kids or adults. Make a chart of everyone's results. What do your results tell you? Do you see a connection between a person's age and how fast he or she breathes?

3. Try to figure out a way to test pets. (Hint: Dogs pant. A cat's body rises up and down as it sleeps.) Which animal breathes more in a minute—a dog, a cat, or a hamster? Do these animals breathe more or less often than people?

What you need:
• a clock or a stopwatch

Air in a Bag *(from page 7)*

Air makes the pieces of paper swirl like confetti, and it makes the bag blow up.

Air Bubbles *(from page 11)*

Air is a gas. It weighs less than water. So air in the water bubbles up to the surface.

Bigger Ears *(from page 25)*

Things sound louder when you cup your hands around your ears. Your cupped hands help your ears catch more sound waves than your ears do by themselves.

Glossary

air—the mixture of gases that surrounds Earth; what we breathe to stay alive

bubbles—small balls of gas inside a liquid

float—to rest on top of air or water

gas—a substance such as air that spreads to fill any space; most gases are invisible

wind—moving air

To Find Out More

At the Library

Bradley, Kimberly Brubaker. *Pop! A Book About Bubbles*. New York: HarperCollins Publishers, 2001.

Branley, Franklyn M. *Air Is All Around You*. New York: HarperTrophy, 1999.

Curry, Don L. *How Do Your Lungs Work?* New York: Children's Press, 2003.

Stille, Darlene. *Air: Inside, Outside, and All Around*. Minneapolis: Picture Window Books, 2004.

On the Web

For more information on air, use FactHound to track down Web sites related to this book.

1. Go to *www.facthound.com*

2. Type in a search word related to this book or this book ID: 0756506387.

3. Click on the *Fetch It* button.

Your trusty FactHound will fetch the best Web sites for you!

Index

animals, 29

balloons, 13, 18
basketball, 7
bicycle pump, 18
blowing, 4, 17, 28
breath, 21, 22, 28, 29
bubbles, 11, 30

ears, 25, 30
electricity, 15, 28

feeling air, 4
floating, 13, 22

helium, 13

kite, 26–27

sailboat, 28
sky, 4
smells, 22
sound waves, 25, 30
sun, 14

tires, 7

water, 8, 11, 21, 30
wind, 14, 17, 26, 28
wind farms, 15
windmills, 15, 28

About the Author

Melissa Stewart earned a bachelor's degree in biology from Union College and a master's degree in science and environmental journalism from New York University. After editing children's science books for nearly a decade, she decided to focus on writing. She has written more than 50 science books for children and contributed articles to *ChemMatters, Instructor, MATH, National Geographic World, Natural New England, Odyssey, Ranger Rick, Science World*, and *Wild Outdoor World*. She also teaches writing workshops and develops hands-on science programs for schools near her home in Northborough, Massachusetts.